Explore the Solar System

Mercury
and
Venus

WORLD
BOOK

a Scott Fetzer company
Chicago
www.worldbookonline.com

World Book, Inc.
233 N. Michigan Avenue
Chicago, IL 60601.
U.S.A.

For information about other World Book publications, visit
our Web site at **http://www.worldbookonline.com** or call
1-800-WORLDBK (967-5325).

For information about sales to schools and
libraries, call **1-800-975-3250 (United States),**
or **1-800-837-5365 (Canada).**

Library of Congress Cataloging-in-Publication Data
Mercury and Venus.
    p. cm. -- (Explore the solar system)
  Summary: "An introduction to Mercury and Venus for
primary and intermediate grade students with information
about their features and exploration. Includes charts and
diagrams, a list of highlights for each chapter, fun facts,
glossary, resource list, and index"--Provided by publisher.
  ISBN 978-0-7166-9534-9
  1. Mercury (Planet)--Juvenile literature. 2. Venus
(Planet)--Juvenile literature. 3. Solar system--Juvenile
literature. I. World Book, Inc.
QB611.M472 2010
523.41--dc22

                         2009029412

ISBN 978-0-7166-9533-2 (set)

Printed in China by Leo Paper Products Ltd.,
  Heshan, Guangdong
1st printing August 2010

Staff
Executive Committee
Vice President and Chief Financial Officer:
  Donald D. Keller
Vice President and Editor in Chief: Paul A. Kobasa
Vice President, Licensing & Business Development:
  Richard Flower
Chief Technology Officer: Tim Hardy
Managing Director, International: Benjamin Hinton
Director, Human Resources: Bev Ecker

Editorial:
Associate Director, Supplementary Publications:
  Scott Thomas
Managing Editor, Supplementary Publications:
  Barbara A. Mayes
Senior Editor, Supplementary Publications:
  Kristina A. Vaicikonis
Manager, Research, Supplementary Publications:
  Cheryl Graham
Manager, Contracts & Compliance
  (Rights & Permissions): Loranne K. Shields
Editor: Michael DuRoss
Writer: Alfred J. Smuskiewicz
Indexer: David Pofelski

Graphics and Design:
Manager: Tom Evans
Coordinator, Design Development
  and Production: Brenda B. Tropinski
Contributing Photographs Editor: Carol Parden

Pre-Press and Manufacturing:
Director: Carma Fazio
Manufacturing Manager: Steven K. Hueppchen
Production/Technology Manager: Anne Fritzinger
Proofreader: Emilie Schrage

Picture Acknowledgments:
Cover front: NASA/Mariner 10/Astrogeology Team/U.S. Geological Survey;
NASA/Magellan Project/JPL; WORLD BOOK illustration by Paul Perreault;
Cover back: NASA/JPL-Caltech/UCLA.

Mercury Attaching His Winged Sandals (1744), marble sculpture by Jean-Baptiste
Pigalle, Louvre, Paris (Bridgeman Art Library) 23; *Venus Crouching* (1686), marble
sculpture by Antoine Coysevox, Louvre, Pars (Bridgeman Art Library) 53; ESA 38, 39, 57;
© Calvin J. Hamilton 11, 37; Hinode JAXA/NASA/PRARC 44; NASA 8, 13, 21, 26, 27, 28,
40, 44, 47, 50, 59; NASA/John Hopkins/Carnegie Institute 20; NASA/JPL/USGS 34, 49;
© John Chumack, Photo Researchers 15; © Frank Zullo, Photo Researchers 25, 55;
© Shutterstock 16, 42.

WORLD BOOK illustrations by Steve Karp 4, 30; WORLD BOOK illustrations by
Paul Perreault, title page, 7, 19, 33, 45.

Astronomers use different kinds of photos to learn about such objects in space as
planets. Many photos show an object's natural color. Other photos use false colors.
Some false-color images show types of light the human eye cannot normally see. Others
have colors that were changed to highlight important features. When appropriate, the
captions in this book state whether a photo uses natural or false color.

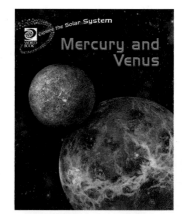

Cover image:
Mercury (left), the smallest
planet in the solar system, and
Venus, the brightest planet in
Earth's night sky, orbit closer to
the sun than any other planets.

Contents

If a word is printed in **bold letters that look like this,** you will find the word's meaning in the glossary on pages 60-61.

Where Is Mercury?

Mercury is the **planet** closest to the sun in the **solar system.**

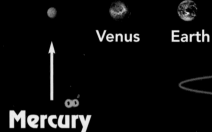

Sun

Venus Earth Mars

Mercury

Jupiter

Mercury is one of the four inner, rocky planets. The other inner planets are Venus, Earth, and Mars. Mercury's **orbit** is between the sun and the orbit of Venus.

Mercury's distance from the sun changes during the year because it follows an **elliptical** (oval-shaped) orbit around the sun. On average, Mercury is about 36 million miles (58 million kilometers) from the sun. In comparison,

Mercury's location in the solar system
(Planets are shown to scale.)

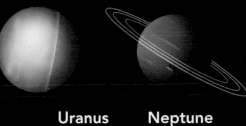

Saturn

Uranus   **Neptune**

Earth is about 93 million miles (150 million kilometers) from the sun. Mercury is about three times as close to the sun as Earth.

At times, Mercury and Earth are only about 48 million miles (77.3 million kilometers) apart. If a jet airplane could fly through space— at 500 miles (800 kilometers) per hour—it would take about 11 years for it to reach Mercury.

Highlights

- Mercury is closer to the sun than any other planet in the solar system.
- Mercury's orbit lies between the sun and the orbit of Venus.
- Mercury's average distance from the sun is about 36 million miles (58 million kilometers).

How Big Is Mercury?

Mercury is the smallest of the eight **planets** in the **solar system.** Mercury is even smaller than Saturn's **moon** Titan (*TY tuhn*) or Jupiter's moon Ganymede (*GAN uh meed*). At its **equator,** Mercury has a **diameter** of 3,032 miles (4,879 kilometers).

Mercury is a little larger than Earth's **moon.** The moon is 2,159 miles (3,474 kilometers) in diameter. Mercury is less than half the size of Earth.

Mercury's small size is one reason it is hard to see from Earth. Mercury usually appears as a tiny dot of light in Earth's night sky.

Mercury is less than half the size of Earth.

Mercury's diameter
3,032 miles (4,879 kilometers)

Earth's diameter
7,926 miles (12,756 kilometers)

What Does Mercury Look Like?

The surface of Mercury is dotted with craters. The large Caloris Basin appears in yellow in a false-color photograph.

Mercury is a small, rocky world covered with many round **craters.** These craters were formed when large **meteorites** crashed into the **planet.**

When seen through a telescope, Mercury seems to change in shape and size from night to night, the way Earth's **moon** does. These apparent changes are called **phases.**

Mercury has phases because different parts of its sunlit side can be seen at different times. The phases depend on whether Mercury is moving toward Earth or away from Earth as Mercury travels around the sun.

Sometimes, only a sliver of Mercury's sunlit side can be seen from Earth. This is how the moon looks to us when it is in a crescent phase. At other times, Mercury's entire sunlit side can be seen. This is how the moon looks to us when it is full.

Highlights

- Mercury is covered with many round craters.
- The craters were formed when meteorites crashed into the planet.
- When seen through a telescope, Mercury seems to change in shape and size from night to night. These changes are called phases.

What Is Mercury Made Of?

Mercury is mostly a big ball of iron. It has a thin layer of **minerals** on its surface. This layer is called the **crust.** Under the crust is a thin, rocky layer called the **mantle.** The mantle may be hot enough to have partly **molten** (melted) rocks.

Beneath the mantle, in the center of the **planet,** is a large iron **core.** Mercury's core takes up about 75 percent of the inside of the planet, much more than Earth's core does. The outer part of Mercury's core is made of flowing hot, molten iron and other substances.

The flowing iron deep in the core conducts electric current. This could explain why Mercury has a **magnetic field.** This field bends the paths of electrically charged particles coming from the sun. The Mariner 10 space **probe,** launched by the United States National Aeronautics and Space Administration (NASA) in 1973, first detected Mercury's magnetic field.

Highlights

- Mercury's surface, called the crust, is made of a thin layer of minerals.
- Underneath the crust is a thin, rocky layer called the mantle.
- The center of Mercury is a large iron core.
- Flowing currents in Mercury's iron core may explain why the planet has a magnetic field.

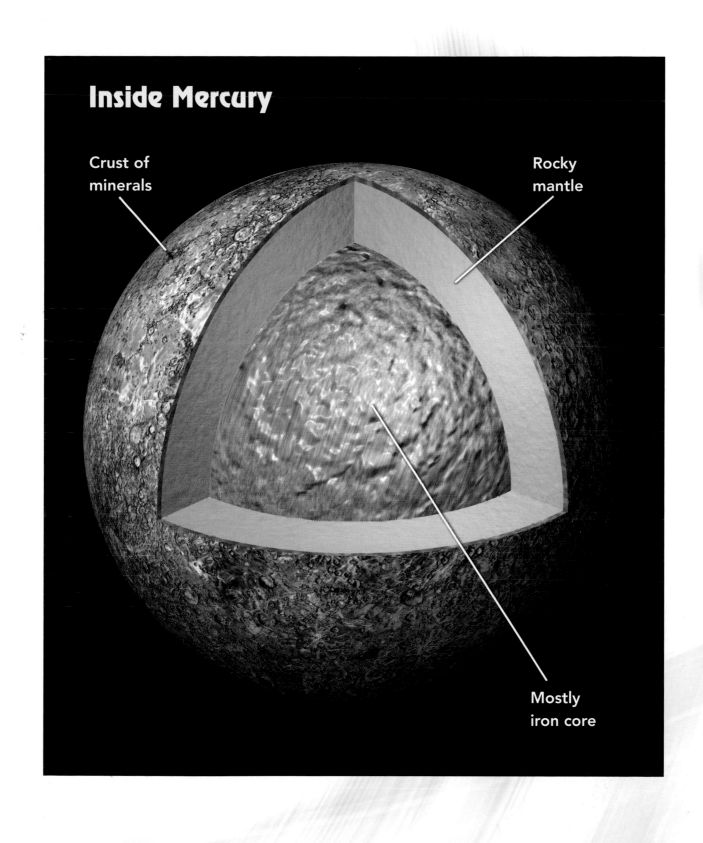

Inside Mercury

Crust of
minerals

Rocky
mantle

Mostly
iron core

What Is Mercury's Atmosphere Made Of?

The Mariner 10 space **probe** found that Mercury is nearly airless, like Earth's **moon.** Several chemical elements form a very thin **atmosphere**. These elements include calcium, **helium, hydrogen,** and sodium. Mercury's atmosphere also has a little oxygen—but not enough for an animal to breathe.

Some scientists think that Mercury may have had a thicker atmosphere billions of years ago. One reason the planet's atmosphere might have become thin could be its small size. Because it is so small, Mercury has only a weak force of **gravity.** Mercury's gravity may not have been strong enough to hold onto any gases in an early atmosphere. Over time, the gases would have scattered into space.

Highlights

- Mercury is almost airless, like Earth's moon.
- The planet has a thin atmosphere, made up of calcium, helium, hydrogen, magnesium, sodium, and a tiny bit of oxygen.
- Mercury may have had a thicker atmosphere billions of year ago that disappeared because the planet's gravity was too weak to hold onto it.

Mercury has almost no atmosphere. Its gravity was probably too weak to hold on to any atmosphere it might have had.

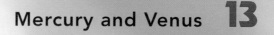

What Is the Weather Like on Mercury?

Mercury is known for its extreme temperatures. The **planet** is both very hot and very cold!

Because Mercury is so close to the sun, the solar rays that reach the planet are about seven times as strong as the rays that reach Earth. In addition, Mercury has few gases in its **atmosphere.** These gases are too thin to reduce the heat and light Mercury receives from the sun. This makes the **daytime** on the planet very hot. The temperature on Mercury can reach 840 °F (450 °C).

In contrast, nighttime is very cold. Then, temperatures can drop as low as –275 °F (–170 °C). Mercury gets so cold because the atmosphere is too thin to

Highlights

- Mercury can be very hot and very cold.
- The temperature on Mercury during the daytime can reach 840 °F (450 °C).
- The temperature on Mercury during the nighttime can reach –275 °F (–170 °C).
- Mercury is very dry, with no rain or snow.

trap the heat that beats down on the planet during the day. The heat escapes into space as soon as the sun sets.

Mercury is also very dry, with no rain or snow. Clouds never form on Mercury, and the sky is always perfectly clear. Mercury's sky is also black, even when the sun is shining. Earth's sky is blue because gas particles in our thick atmosphere scatter the blue light in sunlight throughout the sky. But Mercury's atmosphere is so thin that light waves of all colors travel straight to the surface, leaving the sky black.

Fun Fact

Even though Mercury is the planet closest to the sun, it is not the hottest planet—Venus is.

Mercury   Sun

Mercury crosses in front of the sun in a photograph made through a telescope.

How Does Mercury Compare with Earth?

Mercury's **mass** is much smaller than the mass of Earth. (Mass is the amount of matter in an object.) Because Mercury is less massive, its **gravity** is about one-third as strong as Earth's gravity. Weight depends on gravity. So if you weighed 100 pounds (45 kilograms) on Earth, you would weigh only about 38 pounds (the equivalent of 17 kilograms) on Mercury.

Although Mercury is less massive than Earth, it is nearly as dense because of its huge iron core. (**Density** is the mass of a substance in a given space.) So, a chunk of Mercury would weigh only a bit less than an equal-sized chunk of Earth.

Highlights

- Mercury is much smaller than Earth but nearly as dense.
- Earth is nearly three times farther from the sun than Mercury.
- Mercury's gravity is about one-third as strong as Earth's.
- Mercury has no moons.

How Do They Compare?

	Earth	Mercury
Size in diameter (at equator)	7,926 miles (12,756 kilometers)	3,032 miles (4,879 kilometers)
Average distance from sun	About 93 million miles (150 million kilometers)	About 36 million miles (58 million kilometers)
Length of year (in Earth days)	365.25 days	87.969 days
Length of day (in Earth time)	24 hours	176 Earth days
What an object would weigh ...	If it weighed 100 pounds (45 kilograms) on Earth ...	... it would weigh about 38 pounds (the equivalent of 17 kilograms) on Mercury.
Number of moons	1	0
Rings	No	No
Atmosphere	Nitrogen, oxygen, argon	Calcium, helium, hydrogen, oxygen, potassium, and sodium

How Does Mercury Move Around the Sun?

Mercury **rotates** (spins around) very slowly on its **axis.** (The axis is the imaginary line through the center of a **planet** on which a planet seems to turn.) But Mercury also **orbits** very quickly around the sun. This leads to something unusual about Mercury. Mercury's **day** is twice as long as its **year!**

Mercury takes 59 Earth days to rotate once on its axis. During its rotation, it completes ⅔ of its orbit around the sun. So a day on Mercury equals 176 Earth days.

Mercury orbits the sun about once every 88 Earth days. That means a year on Mercury is only 88 days on Earth.

Highlights

- Mercury spins very slowly on its axis.
- The planet moves very quickly around the sun.
- Mercury's day is equal to about 176 Earth days.
- Mercury's year is equal to about 88 Earth days.

The Orbit and Rotation of Mercury

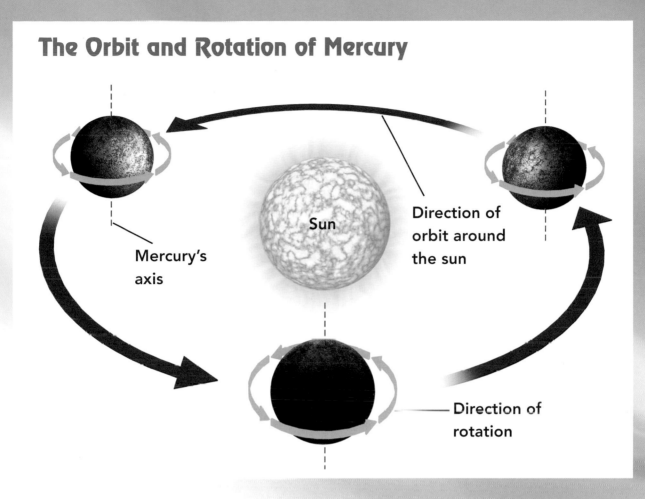

Mercury's axis

Sun

Direction of orbit around the sun

Direction of rotation

Mercury follows an **elliptical** (oval-shaped) orbit around the sun. It moves around the sun faster than any other planet in the **solar system**. Mercury races along its orbit at about 30 miles (48 kilometers) per second. If Mercury did not move that fast, it would fall into the sun. Earth moves much more slowly in its orbit. Earth travels around the sun at about 18.5 miles (30 kilometers) per second.

Why Does Mercury Have So Many Craters?

Photographs taken by NASA's Mariner 10 space **probe** showed many deep **craters** dotting Mercury's surface. These craters formed when **meteorites** crashed into the **planet.** Mercury does not have enough **atmosphere** to burn up meteorites before they hit the surface. The largest crater on Mercury, Caloris Basin, is about 800 miles (1,300 kilometers) wide. This crater is hundreds of miles wider than the largest craters on Earth.

The photos from Mariner 10 also showed mountains and long cliffs. Scientists think the cliffs formed billions of years ago. At that time, the planet may have cooled. Its outer **crust** may have shrunk and buckled.

NASA's Messenger spacecraft photographed an area of Mercury in 2009 that showed volcanic activity (white area) only about 1 billion years old, much more recent than scientists had expected.

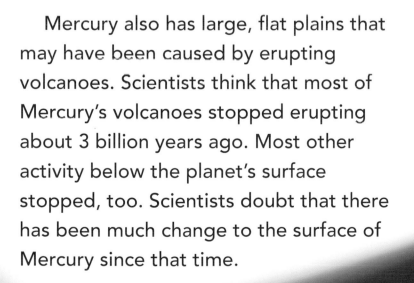

Some of Mercury's craters (see arrows) were flooded with lava that became solid.

Mercury also has large, flat plains that may have been caused by erupting volcanoes. Scientists think that most of Mercury's volcanoes stopped erupting about 3 billion years ago. Most other activity below the planet's surface stopped, too. Scientists doubt that there has been much change to the surface of Mercury since that time.

How Did Mercury Get Its Name?

Thousands of years ago, people noticed a "star" that always seemed to follow the sun in the sky. The object could be seen low in the sky just before sunrise and again just after sunset. Some people thought the object they saw in the morning and the one they saw in the evening were two different objects. Eventually, the ancient Greeks realized that these two "stars" were actually a single **planet.**

Highlights

- The ancient Greeks were the first to realize that what they thought were two stars in the morning and evening sky were really a single planet.

- The ancient Romans named the planet Mercury after the speedy messenger of the gods.

The planet seemed to move across the sky so quickly from one night to the next that the Romans named it after Mercury, the speedy messenger of the gods. In Roman **mythology** (certain types of legends or stories), Mercury wore winged sandals and a winged hat to speed his flight.

A statue of the Roman god Mercury

J-B PIGALLE (1714-1785)
Mercure attachant ses talonnières
Morceau de réception à l'Académie

Where Is Mercury in Earth's Sky?

It is not easy to see Mercury. Mercury is always near the sun, so it often gets lost in the twilight glow of sunset or in the light of sunrise.

When the sky is clear, look for what appears to be a medium-bright star low in the west just after sunset or low in the east just before sunrise. (If you see what appears to be a very bright star in these parts of the sky, however, that is probably Venus.) Mercury is in the west when it is moving toward Earth. It is in the east when it is moving away from Earth. When Mercury is on the opposite side of the sun from Earth, you will not be able to see it.

Highlights

- Mercury is hard to see because it is so small and close to the sun.
- The planet looks like a medium-bright star low in the west right after sunset or low in the east just before sunrise.

Mercury

Mercury in the
sky at sunrise

It is best to use a telescope to look at
Mercury. You will then be able to see that
the **planet** seems to change its shape from
night to night. From one **day** to the next,
different parts of Mercury's sunlit side
become visible from Earth. These changes,
called **phases,** are like those of the **moon.**

Which Space Missions Have Studied Mercury?

Mercury has been studied by only a few space **probes**, compared with Venus and Mars. Only two missions have reached the closest **planet** to the sun.

NASA's Mariner 10 flew past Mercury in 1974 and 1975. A camera on this robotic space probe photographed about half of Mercury's surface. Another instrument on Mariner 10 detected the planet's **magnetic field.**

Mariner 10 taught **astronomers** a lot about Mercury. But it also helped scientists learn how to design even better space probes to send to the other planets.

An artist's drawing of Mariner 10

Highlights

- Mariner 10 flew past Mercury in 1974 and 1975 and was the first space probe to reach the planet.
- It was not until 2008 that a second spacecraft, Messenger, reached Mercury.

In 2004, NASA launched a space probe named Messenger. This probe reached Mercury in 2008. The craft flew by twice and photographed areas of the planet's surface that had never been seen by a spacecraft.

NASA's Messenger probe (shown in an artist's drawing) reaches Mercury in 2008.

Messenger flew by Mercury again in 2009. It was scheduled to go into orbit around the planet in 2011. The probe was to orbit Mercury for one Earth **year** and map its surface in greater detail. It was also to study the planet's minerals, interior, and magnetic field.

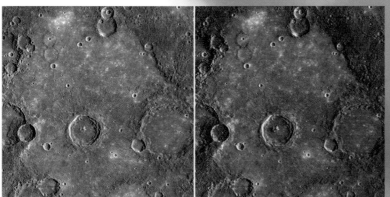

Messenger photos of the planet Mercury appear in black and white (far left) and in false color (left). Scientists add color to such photographs to highlight scientific details.

Could There Be Life on Mercury?

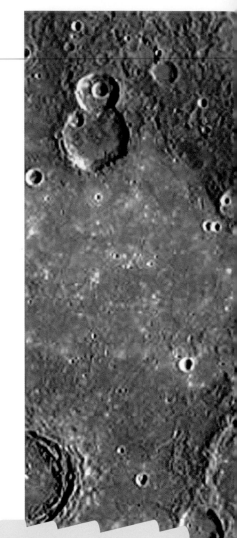

Mercury is one of the most uninviting **planets** in the **solar system.** The scorching daytime temperatures on Mercury would likely make it impossible for life as we know it to survive on the planet.

In addition, no life forms we know of could exist in Mercury's thin **atmosphere**. As far as we know, life forms cannot develop in a **vacuum,** and Mercury's atmosphere comes close to being empty space. Also, Mercury's thin atmosphere allows dangerous solar rays to reach Mercury's surface. These rays would quickly kill most living organisms on the surface.

Highlights

- Mercury's scorching daytime temperatures make it unlikely that life could survive on the planet.
- No life forms we know of could exist in Mercury's thin atmosphere.

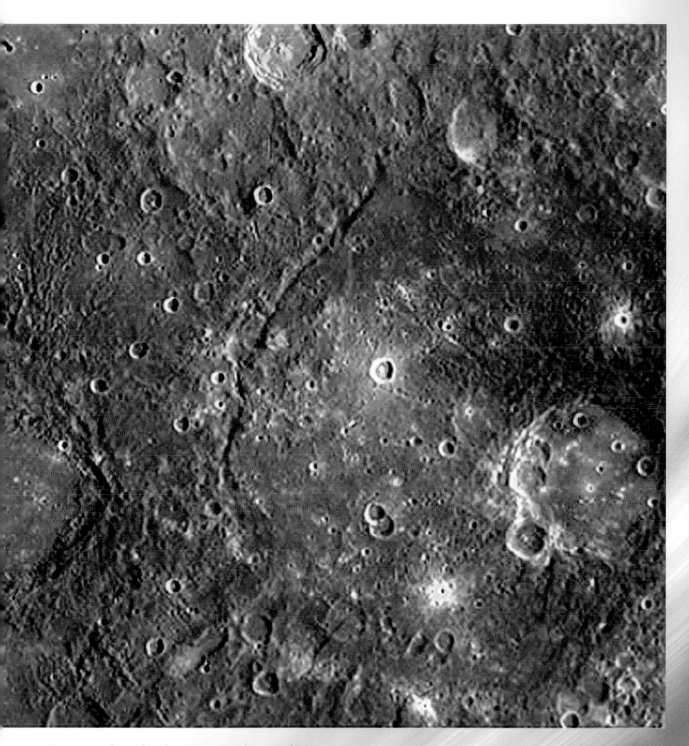

Craters dot the barren surface of Mercury in a false-color photograph taken by the Messenger probe.

Where Is Venus?

Venus is the second **planet** from the sun in the solar system.

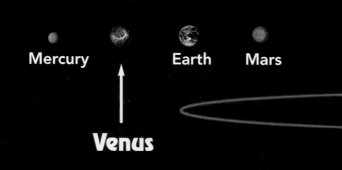

Jupiter

Sun   **Mercury**   **Earth**   **Mars**

Venus

Venus is one of the inner, rocky planets. The other inner planets are Mercury, Earth, and Mars. Venus's **orbit** is between the orbits of Earth and Mercury.

Venus's orbit is more circular than the orbits of other planets in the solar system. On average, Venus orbits about 67 million miles (108 million kilometers) from the sun. In comparison, Earth is about 93 million miles (150 million kilometers) from the sun.

Venus's location in the solar system
(Planets are shown to scale.)

Saturn

Uranus   **Neptune**

About every 19 months, Venus's orbit brings it nearer to Earth. No other planet ever comes closer to Earth than Venus. At their closest, the two planets are about 24 million miles (38 million kilometers) apart. If a jet airplane could fly through space—at 500 miles (800 kilometers) per hour—it would take about 5 ½ years for it to reach Venus.

Highlights

- Venus is the second planet from the sun.

- Its orbit lies between those of Mercury and Earth.

- Venus's average distance from the sun is about 67 million miles (108 million kilometers).

How Big Is Venus?

Venus is sometimes called "Earth's twin" because both **planets** are about the same size. Venus is 7,521 miles (12,104 kilometers) in **diameter** at its **equator**. Earth's diameter is only about 400 miles (644 kilometers) greater.

Fun Fact

Venus appears so bright in the sky that it is often called the Morning Star and the Evening Star.

Highlights

- Venus is about the same size as Earth.
- The diameter of Venus is 7,521 miles (12,104 kilometers).
- Venus and Earth are the largest of the four inner planets, but they are much smaller than the gas giants Jupiter and Saturn.

Venus and Earth are the largest of the four rocky, inner planets that **orbit** near the sun. But Venus and Earth are small when compared to such outer **gas giants** as Jupiter and Saturn. The diameter of Saturn, for example, is about 10 times as large as that of Venus.

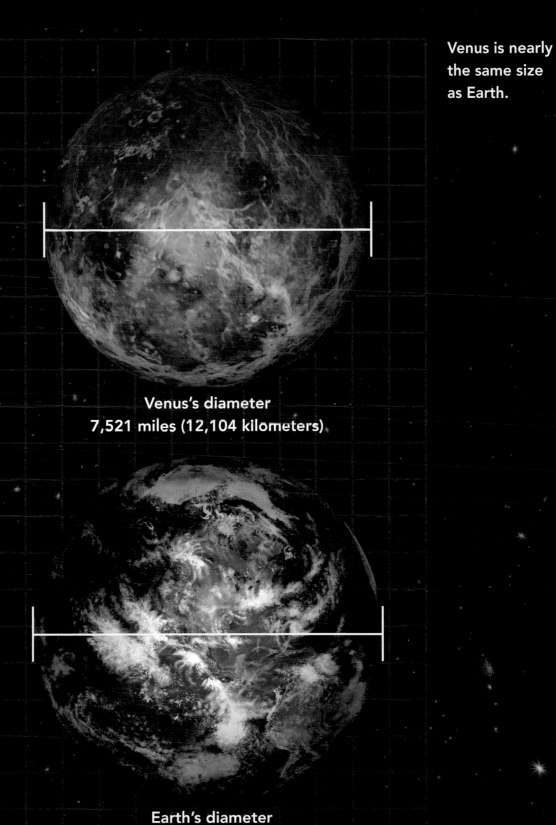

Venus is nearly
the same size
as Earth.

Venus's diameter
7,521 miles (12,104 kilometers)

Earth's diameter
7,926 miles (12,756 kilometers)

What Does Venus Look Like?

Venus is completely covered in thick, swirling, poisonous yellowish clouds. Through a telescope, Venus appears as a bright, yellowish object.

Venus is brighter than any other **planet** or star in Earth's night sky. Venus—like Earth's **moon** and Mercury—appears to change in shape and size from night to night. Such apparent changes are called **phases**. The phases occur because different parts of Venus's sunlit side are visible from Earth at different times.

Venus appears in a false-color photo made up of images taken by several spacecraft and telescopes. Purple, blue, and green areas are generally the lowest areas on the planet. Orange and yellow are higher areas, and red and pink show the highest points.

Highlights

- When viewed from Earth, Venus is brighter than any other planet in the sky.
- Venus is covered in thick, swirling yellowish clouds.
- Venus's surface has craters, volcanoes, mountains, canyons, and large, flat plains.

Venus's blanket of clouds kept scientists from learning much about its surface until space **probes** from the United States and the Soviet Union (now Russia) flew there. Some of these probes landed on Venus and photographed its surface. Scientists discovered that Venus has volcanoes, mountains, canyons, and large, flat plains.

When viewed from Earth, Venus appears to change shape from night to night. Such changes, called phases, occur as different parts of Venus's sunlit side become visible.

Venus

Sun

Earth

What Is Venus Made Of?

The inside of Venus is probably much like the inside of Earth. Scientists think that beneath the rocky, solid **crust,** there may be a rocky, partly **molten** (melted) **mantle.** Beneath the mantle, Venus has a **core** that is most likely made up of **iron.** This iron core may be molten, partially molten, or completely solid. Some scientists think that Venus has a molten outer core and a solid inner core.

The flow of liquid metals in Earth's outer core creates a **magnetic field** around Earth. This field acts like a giant bar magnet. If Venus also has a flowing metal outer core, it should also have a magnetic field. However, space **probes** have found no evidence of a magnetic field around Venus. Scientists are not sure why. Many think that something in Venus's core must be different from Earth's core.

Highlights

- Venus has a rocky, solid crust.
- Under the crust, scientists think there may be a rocky, partly molten (melted) mantle.
- Venus's core is most likely made up of iron, like Earth's core.
- Venus does not seem to have a magnetic field.

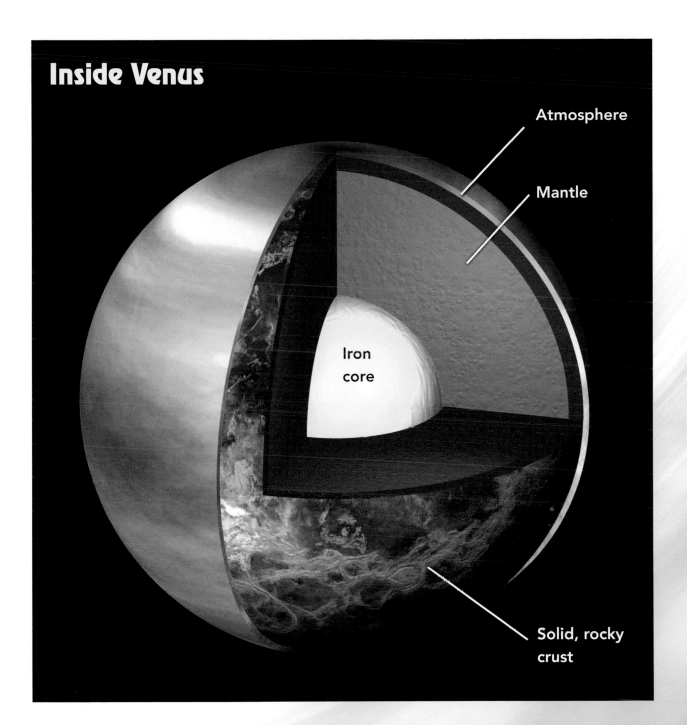

Inside Venus

Atmosphere

Mantle

Iron
core

Solid, rocky
crust

What Is Venus's Atmosphere Made Of?

The **atmosphere** of Venus is made up mostly of a gas called **carbon dioxide.** The atmosphere also contains small amounts of argon, nitrogen, and other substances.

Highlights

- Venus's atmosphere is made up mostly of a gas called carbon dioxide. It also has small amounts of argon, nitrogen, and other substances.

- Venus's atmosphere is very thick and heavy.

- Three layers of thick clouds float in Venus's atmosphere.

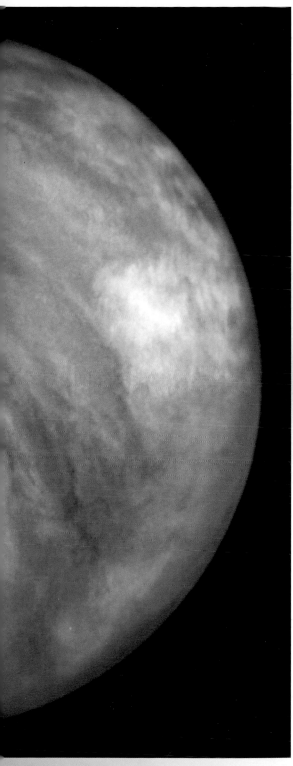

The atmosphere around Venus is very different from the atmosphere around Earth. Venus's atmosphere is much thicker and heavier. The weight of the atmosphere presses down on the **planet's** surface with incredible **pressure.** In fact, the atmospheric pressure at ground level on Venus is about 100 times as great as the pressure at sea level on Earth. Such pressure would quickly crush a human being.

At least three layers of thick clouds float in Venus's atmosphere. These clouds are made of droplets of **sulfuric acid,** the same kind of acid used in car batteries. Sulfuric acid is so strong that it can dissolve metals. Scientists think these clouds formed from chemicals that were released by volcanoes on the planet's surface.

High-speed winds create long clouds on Venus that often stretch for miles (above and in greater detail at right).

What Is the Weather Like on Venus?

The weather on Venus is very hot—even hotter than the weather on Mercury. That is because Venus's thick **atmosphere** traps heat near the surface—much like a greenhouse traps heat to warm plants on Earth. Temperatures during a typical **day** on Venus reach about 870 °F (465 °C).

It is too hot for water to exist on Venus. But findings by NASA space **probes** have led scientists to think that "rain" —made of **sulfuric acid**— falls within Venus's clouds. Heat causes these drops to *evaporate* (change from a liquid to a gas) before they reach the **planet's** surface.

Fun Fact

Studies by NASA scientists of Venus's high temperatures and carbon dioxide atmosphere are helping researchers learn more about global warming on Earth.

Winds often blow at speeds of more than 200 miles (320 kilometers) per hour at the cloud tops of Venus. That is about the speed of strong hurricane winds on Earth. Winds at Venus's surface are much more gentle, blowing at about the speed of a person walking slowly.

Images captured by space probes suggest that lightning may be common on Venus. But scientists are not sure about this.

Highlights

- The weather on Venus is even hotter than on Mercury.

- During a typical day, temperatures on Venus reach about 870 °F (465 °C).

- It is too hot for water to exist on Venus.

- Raindrops made of sulfuric acid fall within Venus's clouds.

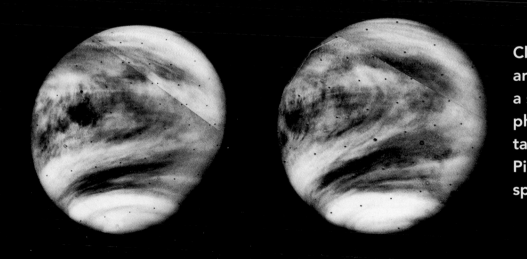

Clouds swirl around Venus in a series of photographs taken by the Pioneer Venus I spacecraft.

How Does Venus Compare with Earth?

Venus and Earth are alike in a few ways. Besides being about the same size, the two **planets** have about the same **mass** and **gravity.** So you would weigh about the same on both planets. If you weighed 100 pounds (45 kilograms) on Earth, you would weigh about 91 pounds (the equivalent of 41 kilograms) on Venus.

However, space **probes** have shown that, in most ways, Venus is very different from Earth. In fact, Venus's dry surface, thick **atmosphere,** and superhot weather are extremely different from conditions on Earth.

Scientists believe that about 4 billion years ago, Venus was much more like Earth. Then the sun was not as bright and not as hot as it is today. At that time, Venus could have had mild temperatures, flowing water, and even an ocean. But, as the sun got brighter and hotter over time, Venus also got hotter and more unlike Earth.

How Do They Compare?

	Earth	Venus
Size in diameter (at equator)	7,926 miles (12,756 kilometers)	7,521 miles (12,104 kilometers)
Average distance from sun	About 93 million miles (150 million kilometers)	About 67 million miles (108 million kilometers)
Length of year (in Earth days)	365.25 days	224.7 days
Length of day (in Earth time)	24 hours	243 Earth days
What an object would weigh ...	If it weighed 100 pounds (45 kilograms) on Earth ...	... it would weigh about 91 pounds (the equivalent of 41 kilograms) on Venus.
Number of moons	1	0
Rings	No	No
Atmosphere	Nitrogen, oxygen, argon	Carbon dioxide, nitrogen, water vapor, argon, carbon monoxide, neon, sulfur dioxide

Highlights

- Venus and Earth are about the same size and have about the same gravity.
- Venus's dry surface, thick atmosphere, and exremely hot weather are very different from conditions on Earth.
- Venus has no moons. Earth has one moon.

How Does Venus Move Around the Sun?

Venus is the only **planet** in the **solar system** that **orbits** the sun in an almost perfectly circular path. All the other planets move around the sun in **elliptical** (oval-shaped) orbits. Venus's orbit keeps it roughly 67 million miles (108 million kilometers) away from the sun.

Venus *revolves* (orbits) around the sun at about 22 miles (35 kilometers) per second. It takes the planet 224.7 Earth **days** to orbit the sun once. That is the length of one **year** on Venus.

Venus **rotates** on its **axis** more slowly than any other planet— once every 243 Earth days. That

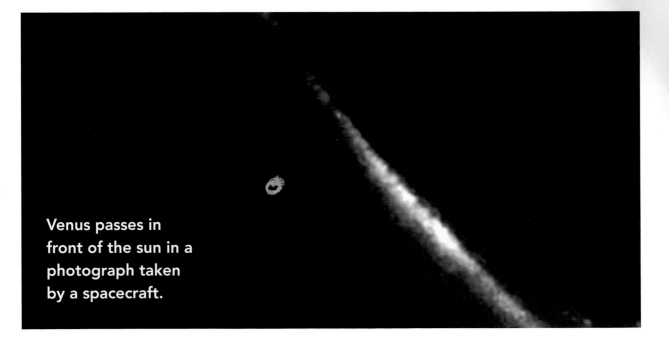

Venus passes in front of the sun in a photograph taken by a spacecraft.

The Orbit and Rotation of Venus

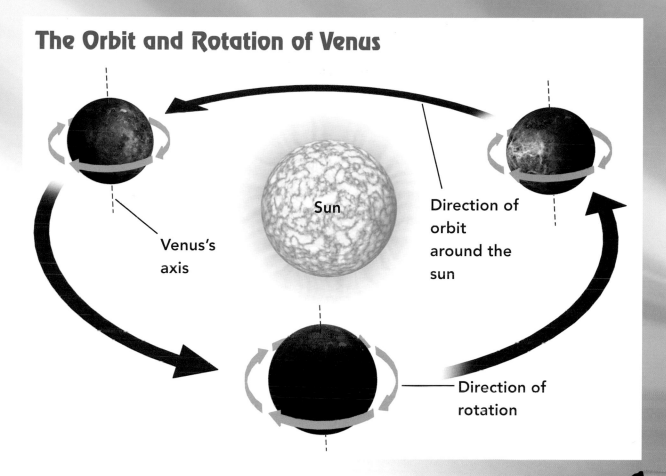

Sun

Venus's axis

Direction of orbit around the sun

Direction of rotation

is the length of a single day on Venus. So, a day on Venus is longer than the planet's year! Like Uranus, Venus does not rotate in the same direction in which it revolves around the sun. All the other planets in the solar system rotate and revolve in the same direction.

Highlights

● Venus is the only planet in the solar system with an almost perfectly circular orbit.

● Venus is one of the few planets that rotate in a clockwise direction but orbit the sun in a counterclockwise one.

● Venus's year is 224.7 Earth days. Its day is 243 Earth days.

What Is the Surface of Venus Like?

Venus's thick **atmosphere** has made it hard for scientists to learn about its surface. They have "explored" the surface using instruments on Earth and on space **probes**.

Like Earth, Venus is a rocky **planet,** so you could stand on the surface. There are thousands of volcanoes of different sizes. Some are as wide as 150 miles (240 kilometers). Overall, Venus is the flattest planet in the inner **solar system.** The planet's plains are covered with cracked, hardened lava. The lava erupted from volcanoes long ago and later cooled and dried. NASA's Magellan spacecraft, which orbited Venus from 1990 to 1994, found long, winding "rivers" of hardened lava. But Venus has no water on its surface.

Some of Venus's features are unlike any found on Earth. Among these are coronae (*kuh ROH nee*) and tesserae (*TEHS uh ree*).

Highlights

- Although Venus is very flat, its surface is covered with thousands of volcanoes.
- The planet has no water, and its plains are covered with hardened lava.
- Venus has unusual features not seen on Earth.

An impact crater on the surface of Venus in a colorized photo

Coronae (the plural of corona) are large, ring-like structures as much as 360 miles (580 kilometers) across. Tesserae (the plural of tessera) are raised areas in which ridges and valleys formed in different directions.

Both coronae and tesserae are evidence of how some of Venus's surface regions move and change over time. Venus also has high mountains and deep **craters** that formed when **meteorites** struck the planet's surface long ago.

Does Venus Have Continents?

On Earth, the continents are large areas of dry land surrounded or nearly surrounded by lower areas that contain water—oceans or seas. Venus has two areas that are like continents. There is no water around them now, but scientists think they may have been surrounded by water in the past. The areas are called Aphrodite Terra (*af ruh DY tee TEHR uh*) and Ishtar Terra (*ISH tahr TEHR uh*).

Aphrodite Terra lies along the **equator**. It has many volcanoes. One of the highest is Maat Mons, which rises 5 miles (8 kilometers) above the surface of Venus. Aphrodite Terra is about the size of South America.

Fun Fact

All of the volcanoes on Venus are named after goddesses from the mythologies of many cultures, from Assyro-Babylonian (Irnini, the goddess of cedar-tree mountains) to Zairian (Woyo, the rainbow goddess).

Ishtar Terra, which is near Venus's North Pole, covers an area about the size of Australia. Ishtar Terra has four large mountain ranges. The highest of these is the Maxwell Montes. The highest point of the Maxwell Montes rises about 7 miles (11.3 kilometers) into the sky. That is more than 1 mile (1.6 kilometers) higher than Mount Everest, the highest place on Earth.

Highlights

- Venus has two continent-like highland areas, Ishtar Terra and Aphrodite Terra.
- Venus's continents are not surrounded by water as the continents on Earth are.

A false-color radar map of Ishtar Terra, one of Venus's highland areas, shows low areas in blues and greens and higher areas in yellows and reds.

Does Venus Have Active Volcanoes?

Volcanic eruptions are one of the main forces that cause change on Earth's surface. The hot lava that erupts from volcanoes flows over the land and covers up older features—almost the way an old road is repaved with asphalt.

Much of the surface of Venus is also "paved" with flows of lava. Most of these flows probably came from volcanoes that erupted more than 500 million years ago, but some may have been more recent. The lava covered up many older **craters.** That is one reason why there are far fewer craters on Venus's surface today than there are on Mercury or Earth's **moon.**

Highlights

- Much of the surface of Venus is covered with lava from volcanoes that erupted millions of years ago.
- Lava has filled many of the craters on Venus.
- Some scientists think there may still be active volcanoes on Venus today.

Do volcanoes still erupt on Venus? Scientists are not sure. Some scientists think that volcanoes on Venus may be active from time to time. Space **probes** have found regions of the **planet's** surface that have changed since the 1990's. Many scientists believe these changes were caused by recent volcanic activity. Space probes have also found certain gases in the **atmosphere** that may have been blown out by volcanoes.

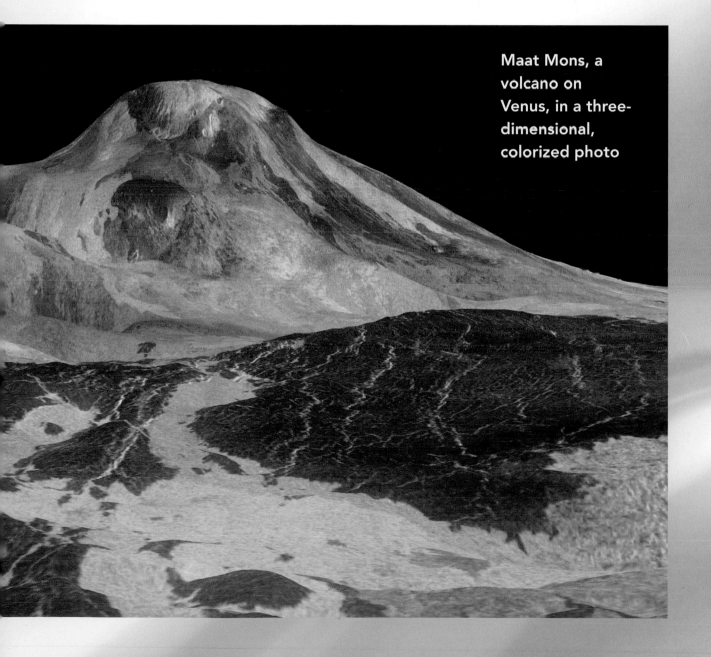

Maat Mons, a volcano on Venus, in a three-dimensional, colorized photo

How Did Venus Get Its Name?

Thousands of years ago, many people thought Venus was two different **planets.** Later, people realized that the bright object seen in the eastern sky at sunrise and the bright object seen in the western sky at sunset were the same single planet.

The dazzling brightness of Venus led people in ancient China to name it Tai-pe, which means *beautiful white one.* The ancient Greeks and Romans linked the planet with **mythological** goddesses. The Romans named it Venus after their goddess of love and beauty.

Highlights

- For many thousands of years, people thought Venus was two different planets.
- The Romans named Venus after their goddess of love and beauty.
- Venus is the only planet named after a female figure.

Venus is the only planet that the Romans named after a female figure. In addition, almost all **craters,** mountains, and other features on Venus are named after real women, mythological women, or goddesses.

The only feature on Venus named for a man is the mountain range Maxwell Montes. It was named for the Scottish scientist James Clerk Maxwell (1831–1879).

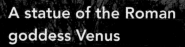

A statue of the Roman goddess Venus

Where Is Venus in Earth's Sky?

Venus is the easiest **planet** to find in the sky, because it is the brightest. Look for what appears to be a very bright star low in the western sky just after sunset, or low in the eastern sky just before sunrise.

When Venus is moving toward Earth, it is in the west. When it is moving away from Earth, it is in the east. When Venus is on the other side of the sun from Earth, it cannot be seen. When Venus is at its brightest point, it can be seen in Earth's **daytime** sky.

If you use a telescope to look at Venus, you will see that the planet appears to change its shape. From night to night, it will go through apparent changes called **phases,** as does Earth's **moon.** You can keep a notebook of your observations and draw sketches of the changing phases of Venus.

Highlights

- Venus is an easy planet to find in the sky because it is so bright.
- Venus appears low in the western sky just after sunset.
- It appears low in the eastern sky just after sunrise.

Venus

Venus and a crescent
moon in the western
sky at sunset

Which Space Missions Have Studied Venus?

Most of what we know about Venus has come from space **probes** that the United States or the former Soviet Union sent to the **planet.** The Soviet Union launched several Venera spacecraft to either fly by or land on Venus in the 1960's, 1970's, and 1980's. The Venera landers

Highlights

- The first spacecraft to reach Venus were the former Soviet Union's Venera spacecraft.
- In 1978, two NASA Pioneer spacecraft reached the planet.
- NASA's Magellan spacecraft explored Venus from 1990 to 1994.
- The European Space Agency's Venus Express began orbiting the planet in 2006.

photographed the surface and made other studies. Some of these spacecraft lasted as long as 110 minutes before the high temperatures and crushing **pressures** on Venus destroyed them.

In 1978, the NASA probes Pioneer Venus 1 and

Fun Fact

NASA probe Mariner 10 became the first spacecraft to visit two planets. It flew past both Mercury and Venus in 1974.

Pioneer Venus 2 reached Venus. Pioneer Venus 1 orbited the planet for nearly 14 years, mapping the surface and studying the **atmosphere.** Pioneer Venus 2 dropped special instruments into the atmosphere that measured such things as temperatures and wind speeds.

In the 1990's, NASA's Magellan spacecraft made detailed images of Venus's surface. The European Space Agency's (ESA) Venus Express probe, launched in 2005, reached Venus in 2006. Venus Express began to analyze the makeup of rocks on the planet and to search for signs of ongoing volcanic activity.

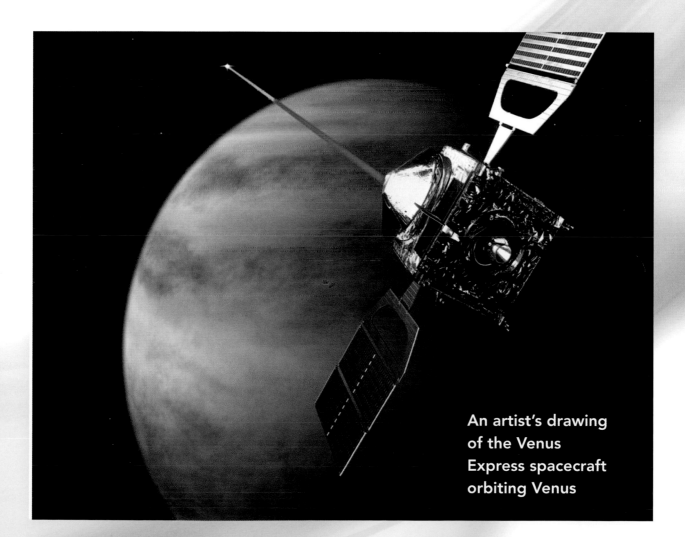

An artist's drawing of the Venus Express spacecraft orbiting Venus

Could There Be Life on Venus?

Venus could not support any form of life known on Earth. In fact, astronauts will almost certainly never even visit Venus. The great heat, poisonous atmosphere, and crushing **pressure** would instantly kill anyone who tried to land there. People may one day visit Mars and perhaps even live there for long periods. But Venus could never support human life.

Before scientists learned what Mars is really like, many people imagined it to be a place filled with "little green men" or other forms of life. As recently as 50 years ago, people had similar ideas about Venus. Because Venus is so close to the sun, some people thought that it might be a warm, swampy paradise, like some tropical places on Earth. They imagined strange creatures running through jungles and swimming in seas.

We now know that those ideas about Venus were wrong. But we can still appreciate the fascinating world that Venus really is.

Highlights

- According to scientists, Venus cannot support any form of life known on Earth because of its high temperatures and pressure and lack of water.
- Decades ago, people thought that Venus was a warm, swampy place and that strange creatures might live there.

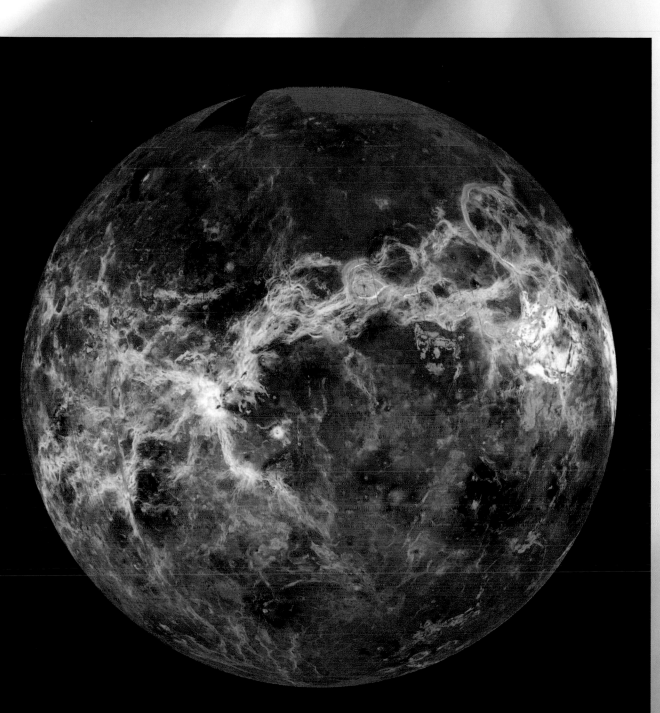

The surface of Venus
in a photo taken
using radar

Glossary

astronomer A scientist who studies stars, planets, and other heavenly bodies.

atmosphere The gases that surround a planet.

axis In planets, the imaginary line on which the planet seems to turn, or rotate. (The axis of Earth is an imaginary line running from the North Pole to the South Pole.)

carbon dioxide A compound formed of carbon and oxygen.

core The center part of the inside of a planet.

crater A bowl-shaped depression on the surface of a moon, a planet, or an asteroid.

crust The solid, outer layer of a planet.

day The time it takes a planet to rotate (spin) once around its axis and come back to the same position in relation to the sun.

density The amount of matter in a given space.

diameter The distance of a straight line through the middle of a circle or a thing shaped like a ball.

elliptical Having the shape of an ellipse, which is like an oval or a flattened circle.

equator An imaginary circle around the middle of a planet.

gas giant Any of four planets— Jupiter, Saturn, Uranus, and Neptune—made mostly of gas and liquid.

gravity The effect of a force of attraction that acts between all objects because of their mass (that is, the amount of matter the objects have).

helium The second most abundant chemical element in the universe.

hydrogen The most abundant chemical element in the universe.

magnetic field The space around a magnet or magnetized object within which its power of attraction works.

mantle The area of a planet between the crust and the core.

mass The amount of matter a thing contains.

meteorite A mass of stone or metal that falls to the surface of a planet without burning up in that planet's atmosphere.

mineral An inorganic (nonliving) substance made up of crystals.

molten Melted.

moon A smaller body that orbits a planet.

mythology Certain types of legends or stories.

orbit The path that a smaller body takes around a larger body, such as the path that a planet takes around the sun.

phases The night-to-night changes an observer on Earth seems to see in the shape and size of the moon or of certain planets. The apparent changes occur as different parts of the moon or planet are lit by the sun and become visible on Earth.

planet A large, round body in space that orbits a star. A planet must have sufficient gravitational pull to clear other objects from the area of its orbit.

pressure The force caused by the weight of a planet's atmosphere as it presses down on the layers below it.

probe An unpiloted device sent to explore space. Most probes send data (information) from space.

rotate To spin around.

solar system The sun and the planets and other heavenly bodies that orbit around the sun.

sulfuric acid A colorless, dense, oily liquid that destroys or eats away at materials with which it comes into contact.

vacuum Space that contains almost no matter.

year The time it takes a planet to complete one orbit around the sun.

For More Information

Books

Hot Planets: Mercury and Venus by David Jeffries (Crabtree Publishing, 2009)

Mercury:

Destination Mercury by Giles Sparrow (PowerKids Press, 2010)

Mercury by Elaine Landau (Children's Press, 2008)

Venus:

Destination Venus by Giles Sparrow (PowerKids Press, 2010)

Venus by Elaine Landau (Children's Press, 2008)

Web sites

Mercury:

NASA's Solar System Exploration: Mercury
http://sse.jpl.nasa.gov

National Geographic's Science and Space: Mercury
http://science.nationalgeographic.com

Venus:

NASA's Solar System Exploration: Venus
http://sse.jpl.nasa.gov

National Geographic's Science and Space: Venus
http://science.nationalgeographic.com

Index